INNOVATION IN SUSTAINABLE HOUSING: TANGO

**Moore Ruble Yudell Architects & Planners
with SWECO FFNS Arkitekter AB**

Essay by Michael Webb

First published in the
United States of America by
Edizioni Press, Inc.
469 West 21st Street
New York, New York 10011
www.edizionipress.com

ISBN: 1-931536-38-4
Library of Congress Catalogue Card Number:
2004116075

Design: Project Projects
Editors: Sarah Palmer, Aaron Seward
Cover Image: Werner Huthmacher

Printed in China

TANGO: DANCING OUT OF THE BOX
BY MICHAEL WEBB

It takes two to tango, and Moore Ruble Yudell partnered with the Swedish firm of **SWECO FFNS Arkitekter AB** to design a project called Tango as their contribution to the 2001 housing exposition in Malmö. The name was inspired by its brilliant hues and dynamic body language. Eight vibrantly colored steel and glass towers dance around a landscaped courtyard, exposing most of the living rooms to the outdoors, with a wall of bedrooms wrapped around three sides of the block. Each of the 27 apartments has a unique character, the block is self-sufficient in energy, and everything from heating to door locks can be individually controlled from a computer keyboard. Tango won the Best Housing Project of the Year award in Sweden as well as a National Honor Award from the AIA, and residents willingly pay up to three times as much per square foot to live there as they would in a more conventional space.

The collaboration between the two architectural firms began in 1987, when an enlightened Malmö developer, **MKB Fastighets AB**, brought them together to design Potatisåkern [1], an upscale complex of 320 apartments inspired by MRY's Tegel Harbor [2] project in Berlin. Built in three phases over the next 15 years, it's a fusion of California informality and Swedish tradition, and its picturesquely massed apartment blocks and villas enclose an expansive green axis. Though much delayed and reduced in size, it proved a great success, bringing the developer profit and esteem. When the city of Malmö announced its plans for "Bo01, City of Tomorrow," MKB was awarded three of the 46 plots on the 50-acre waterfront site, and they commissioned MRY and FFNS to create a model of sustainable design on a block that faces east to the city.

Green architecture has deep roots in Sweden, with its history of frugality and strong technological tradition. Conservation reduces energy costs through the cold, dark winters, and limits pollution. There's an ongoing effort to share benefits equitably. Though the government program to build a million new housing units, launched in the 1960s, was later criticized for producing bland, impersonal blocks, it was an enlightened policy to offer everyone a decent home at a fair price. Expositions, beginning with the Stockholm Fair of 1930, which was designed by Gunnar Asplund to be a showcase of modernism, have provided a testing ground for innovative ideas. Some comprised short-lived temporary structures; others, like the housing expos of 1955 and 1999 in Helsingborg, left an enduring legacy of useful models.

Malmö had special reasons for hosting an exposition in 2001. The newly opened Öresund bridge to Copenhagen made it the first stop in Sweden for land traffic from the European Union, which Sweden joined in 1995. However, the former industrial city of a quarter of a million inhabitants had fallen on hard times. Its shipyard, once the largest in Sweden, shut down in 1979, and heavy industry atrophied. A factory for the assembly of Saab cars was constructed on the waterfront, but it quickly succumbed to a downturn in the economy, and was demolished. In common with other Western port cities, from Newark, New Jersey, to Bilbao in the Basque region of Spain, Malmö is struggling to reinvent itself and redevelop its desolate docklands. One of the goals of Bo01 was to create an inspiring symbol of a new waterfront that will be built out over the next decade, enhancing the quality of life for residents and visitors, and generating badly

1

2

12

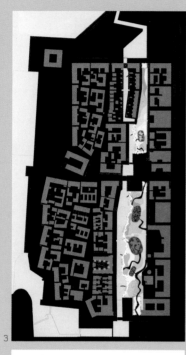

3

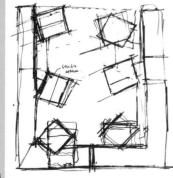

4

needed employment and tax revenues. Eventually, 30,000 people will live and/or work on the 325-acre landfill of the Western Harbor, sandwiched between parks and beaches, the Sound, and a few existing office and factory buildings, a short bicycle ride from the city center.

Bo01 was organized by a non-profit organization, Svensk Bomassa (Swedish Housing Fair), which is jointly owned by the Swedish state, the Swedish Association of Municipalities, the Swedish Association of Municipal Housing Foundations, and a number of cities, including Malmö. Klas Tham, a protégé of architect-urbanist Ralph Erskine, laid out the exposition within the grid of the city's master plan as a tight-knit complex of blocks, almost medieval in its density (3). He looked to the traditional small-scale neighborhoods of Malmö, and the old university town of Lund, for the urban structure within which contemporary architects would provide the urban forms. He sought to combine shelter from winds with a sense of surprise; a lucid plan with a sense of intimacy. "The grid was distorted, partly by the wind, like a fishing net hung up to dry," he observes. "This makes it more rational, more worthy of being lived and strolled in."

Canals and the waterfront promenade define the rectangular site. There's a park to the north and a marina to the south, attracting a steady flow of visitors. The four- to five-story perimeter is built up like a wall and penetrated by narrow walkways and ramps to basement garages. Within the complex, blocks step down in height and open up to landscaped recreational spaces. As the scheme matures, the 522 apartments and 37 houses are being supplemented by workplaces, a school, a library, restaurants, cafés, shops, and daycare

centers. Salt y Brygga, which was established in the first phase, won the best new restaurant in Sweden award.

The theme of the exposition was sustainability. As Tham explained: "The sustainable way of life must show that it can be at least as comfortable, as economically profitable, as secure and pleasant, and as exciting and beautiful as today's unsustainable." To achieve this goal, private developers were extensively briefed and 20 agreed to participate. They were urged to select skilled architects from across Europe. For lack of time and funding, almost everything was designed by Swedish architects, though 11 houses were built as a European village by countries applying to join the EU. Santiago Calatrava's "Turning Torso" apartment tower might have been the signature building of Bo01 but its construction was delayed and it will not be completed until 2005. MRY was the only non-European firm to participate.

"Shock us—and don't worry about the money," said Allan Karlsson, the visionary CEO of MKB, to Bertil Öhström, the project designer for FFNS. Encouraged by this gesture of support, Öhström and his colleague, Lars Lindahl, traveled to Santa Monica for a week-long charette with John Ruble, Buzz Yudell, and James Mary O'Connor of MRY. As O'Connor recalls, "we paired off in different rooms and sketched, exploring the notion of movement within a frame (4). Our Swedish colleagues and we were like a small group of jazz musicians who share a common theme, melody and approach to their art." Ruble remembers that "we tried different ideas, but once we came up with the concept of the wall and the rotating towers, the rest of the week was spent fleshing it out and

13

adding detail, while keeping the diagram clear." The process was interactive, and it yielded a scheme that is a microcosm of the Bo01 plan, with its hard wrapper and its soft interior merging into a protected landscape.

"At the outset, I wished they had given us a site overlooking the Sound, but afterwards I was glad we got the one we did, because the inland environment is not so harsh and allowed a little more flexibility in the design," says Ruble. "The Öresund is rarely a pretty body of water. For much of the year it looks like reclaimed oil, and the winter winds are strong and cold. Only on late summer afternoons does it get the golden glow for which it is named."

The city authorities had originally planned their exposition for 2000; even after moving it back a year they left perilously little time for the participants to refine their designs, secure the necessary approvals, and do a good job of construction. Some of the schemes were rushed to completion, and are neither as inventive nor as well built as the organizers intended. A few architects seemed more concerned to impress visitors than to address the long-term needs of residents, and one block has had to be retrofitted in order to attract tenants. MKB, by contrast, were well organized, and spent what was required to ensure success. The quality of finishes, as well as the complexity of the plan and infrastructure pushed Tango well over its original budget. The firm views it as a long-term investment in the future of Malmö.

A division of responsibility emerged early on and continued through the design-build process. MRY did computer modeling of the exterior (5) and built physical models to show to prospective tenants, and FFNS modeled the interiors. Each critiqued the other's proposals and submitted them for review by Tham and the city building office. Öhström describes how plans and drawings were emailed back and forth, and how FFNS had to master a thick book of city regulations and fight for two months to secure the necessary approvals. The urban design framework was set, but MRY pushed against it (in what Ruble laughingly describes as "their typical fashion") to make some adjustments to the massing of the north and south sides. A request to add a story to the façade was rejected, and the design benefited from that decision.

The architects worked to simplify and enrich the scheme, achieving a syncopated rhythm of window openings and cladding panels in the exterior façades (6). Louvered concrete panels were placed horizontally and vertically. They evoke traditional wood clapboarding and catch the light, but the abstract patterns of concrete and glass, and the shallow projecting bays avoid any sense of a historical pastiche. O'Connor recalls that, "I was playing a lot of checkers with my son during the first month of the design, and the movement of the pieces appears in the plan. However, I was steered away from doing a checkered, two-color façade, since natural light animates the relief and varies the tones of the wall through the day."

For MRY, Tango marked a decisive shift away from the picturesque postmodernism of Tegel and Potatisåkern, where references to tradition and context are overt. They had tried to introduce a sharp-edged, contemporary sensibility in their proposal for the final phase of Potatisåkern, but MKB felt that this would compromise the identity of a project that

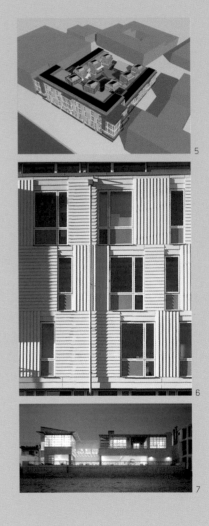

5

6

7

14

8

9

10

11

stood apart from its neighbors yet offered comforting reminders of the past.

In Bo01, the mandate was to be innovative, and that gave the architects the opportunity they sought, to build on the modernist tradition in Sweden and create a building that was referential and progressive, one-of-a-kind yet welcoming. Just as Tegel (conceived in 1980 in the brief heyday of postmodernism) was the seed for much of what the firm did subsequently, so have the crisp forms and jazzy rhythms of **Tango** fed into recent MRY projects, including the **Peg Yorkin house in Malibu** (7), the new **public library** (8) and parking structure in Santa Monica, and the Fresno Courthouse. It marked a paradigm shift away from the style that informed Charles Moore's work when he founded the firm.

The shift is evident in the use of color. When Potatisåkern was being designed, Tina Beebe (MRY's resident expert on color, who honed her skills with the late Ray Eames) traveled through southern Sweden with Öhström in search of inspiration. She remarked on the bold reds and yellows in the rural vernacular, and the way that fishermen painted their houses in brilliant colors (9)—in such villages as Ystad and Simrishamn—so that they could identify them from far out to sea. Even in Malmö, one can find sizzling yellow ochre walls in a half-timbered medieval courtyard. In Potatisåkern, color is applied as traditional washes over large expanses of stucco, and the intensity increases as one progresses from the perimeter to the interior of the development.

For Tango, Beebe conceived the towers as brilliantly colored objects standing apart from each other and set off by a neutral ground, and she tried out different hues on the computer models (10). The Swedish fishing villages were one source, but another, more exotic reference proved decisive with the review committee. O'Connor carried some postcards of La Boca (11)—a working-class barrio in Buenos Aires that residents have turned into a feast of color—into a meeting on a gray day in Malmö, and the response was enthusiastic. Beebe showed them intense blues and greens as part of her palette, but made substitutions in response to the committee's preference for warmer colors.

"It was important that the colors hang together as a set and that each have its own identity," she explains. "The cost of the high-tech curtainwall system for the towers presented a problem. FFNS considered applying color to the plaster walls, leaving the towers white. It was hard to get the eight different colors powder-coated onto the steel frames and glazing bars, but we found a way of doing it." Her insistence paid off: the towers give Tango its identity, bobbing up over the low entry wall and creating a sense of discovery as you turn the corner. Residents have proudly embraced the concept, identifying their apartment by the color of the tower. A random pattern of colored squares enhances the walls of the courtyard, but the exterior façades are a uniform creamy gray.

The crisp, blocky forms of the towers—comparable in their frank use of industrial materials to the Eames house in west Los Angeles—are set off by the landscaping of the courtyard. The concept of an oval island surrounded by plantings was jointly developed by MRY and Karin Bellander of FFNS. As with the colors, there was a divergence of opinion. "Karin liked the idea of an English garden, with flowers and climbing vines," says Beebe. "We wanted it to be gutsy and native, to recreate the wetland that was here before the harbor." They agreed to reduce the diversity of plantings and to emphasize a few silver birches and the grasses, which leach chemicals from the soil of this brownfield site, and absorb the dirt that the rain washes from the roofs (12).

Thus the garden plays a double role: *rus in urbe*, and a mechanism to purify earth and water. The grasses, trees, and accent flowers are naturally irrigated and excess water flows into the canal, without need for chemical or mechanical filters. This communal space serves as a buffer to separate the private decks and balconies. A boardwalk surrounds a central ellipse of gravel and is linked by bridges to the shared entrance of each pair of towers. In America, these walkways would be fenced in to assure safety and avert litigation; the sensible Swedes require only a token handrail.

Another big difference between the two countries is the prevalence of rental apartments in Sweden, and the way that these are designed and maintained with greater care than is given to most market housing in the United States. At the outset of the design process, MKB invited 30 prospective tenants to configure their apartment according to need. The group comprised families, childless couples and singles of different ages, working with spaces that ranged from 650 square feet with one bedroom to 1,950 square feet with three, and ceiling heights from under nine to over 25 feet. There was a general preference for more, though smaller rooms, but each potential renter wanted something different. The intention

was to customize each apartment; however, for lack of time, it was decided to simplify and abstract specific recommendations. Even so, each apartment has a different configuration.

One consistent feature of the Tango apartments is the division between snug bedrooms around the periphery and larger living-dining areas that project into the garden and "borrow" space from the courtyard and views over rooftops to the sea, making them feel even more roomy than they are. The towers range from two and a half to four and a half stories, and contain loft-like spaces at the top. It's exhilarating to stand in a living room and look out to the other colored towers, feeling that one is in one's own private space while catching glimpses of neighbors in theirs. There's a suggestion of Hitchcock's *Rear Window*—though one supposes that the denizens of Malmö are more discreet than New Yorkers in their patterns of behavior. At night, the fully glazed towers glow like lanterns (13).

Steven Joyce, an American business correspondent who moved here from Copenhagen soon after completion, values the sense of community. "It's an island, linked by bridges to the city, and a social condenser, but it's also my home," he says. "I feel secure and comfortable and I can go away without worrying about anything."

Many features contribute to this sense of well-being. Öhström and his colleagues at FFNS seized the opportunity to specify unpretentious good-quality materials and impeccable detailing, and the contractor shared their passion to do things right. Even the smallest rooms are well proportioned, and are given a sense of warmth by the

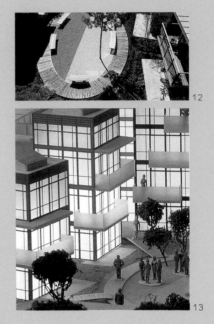

12

13

16

14

industrial-grade knotted maple floors, and built-in cherry cabinetry. White walls are accented in teal blue, salmon, lavender, and five other soft tones. Though miniscule by American standards, the bathrooms are well-appointed, with under-floor heating, three sizes of black ceramic tiles, glass swing doors on the shower, and a wall-hung toilet. Sliding window screens of translucent plastic, banded in cherry, assure privacy. Each apartment is fitted with sprinklers and built-in alarms, and has a 50-square-foot storage cubicle in the basement. A pavilion beside the entry to the courtyard shelters bicycles and trash bins.

The most impressive amenities are out of sight. A wind turbine plant generates electricity. Three thousand square feet of rooftop photovoltaic panels convert solar energy into heat that is fed into the district network. These panels are surrounded by a carpet of mountain grasses—a traditional feature of Scandinavian roofs—which provides insulation, restores oxygen to the atmosphere, and slows run-off from heavy rain. In the triple-glazed windows, the outer space is filled with argon and warm air circulates through the inner. Each apartment has an "intelligent wall" (14) containing wiring, vertical shafts for fiber-optic cables, and mechanical services. These include under-floor hot water channels, heated ceiling panels, and convectors, which also provide cool air in summer. The controls can be accessed by removing a section of cherry wood paneling; however, residents prefer to use their laptops to activate the system from wherever they may be via the building's private service portal. They can adjust utility settings, open windows, lock and unlock their doors, display text on an electronic message board, and even reserve

the community room or guest apartment with a few keystrokes.

As Ruble observes, "This was a rare opportunity to build innovative housing that serves as a social generator with few budgetary constraints. I wish we could do something like this in the United States, but that would require the vision and public investment that we found with MKB and our Swedish partners."

SITE

Bo01, the summer 2001 housing exhibition of which **Tango** is a part, occupies a patch of reclaimed coastal land just at the northwest edge of central Malmö. This former industrial site enjoys an expansive waterfront looking west to Öresund—the Golden Sound. Across the water the citylights of Copenhagen can be seen at night, and crossing the Sound in a ferry on a late summer afternoon can be transcendently beautiful.

WALLED TOWN
Built as a permanent community, the Bo01 project also has to contend with the ten months of the year when Öresund is a windy, wet, cold body of water—a steel-gray seascape that thrashes heavily against a rocky sea wall on the very exposed western edge of the site. With this climate in mind, Bo01 was laid out with a protective perimeter—a four- to five-story wall of housing that provides at least some psychological enclosure for the smaller scale interior blocks and pedestrian streets. Located on the tamer lee-side of the site, **Tango** forms one segment of the town wall.

REGIONAL CHARACTER
In the wider context the historic center of Malmö, as well as the neighboring university town Lund, are wonderful collections of architecture and planning that span several centuries. Early brick and half-timber houses jostle alongside baroque plaster façades and muscular stone fronts from the prosperous 19th and early 20th centuries. The resulting character is surprisingly organic—a play of textures, colors, and forms that accumulate, bringing life to the traditional urban sequences of streets, squares, and parks. Occasional early modernist works possess an unexpected charm. The only real interruptions take the form of bland, repetitive strips of in-fill from the 1960s and 70s.

It was the vigorous collage of materials, elements such as balconies and bay windows, and color, as well as the warmly human scale of these Swedish towns that the architects hoped to continue by more contemporary means in the design of **Tango**.

18

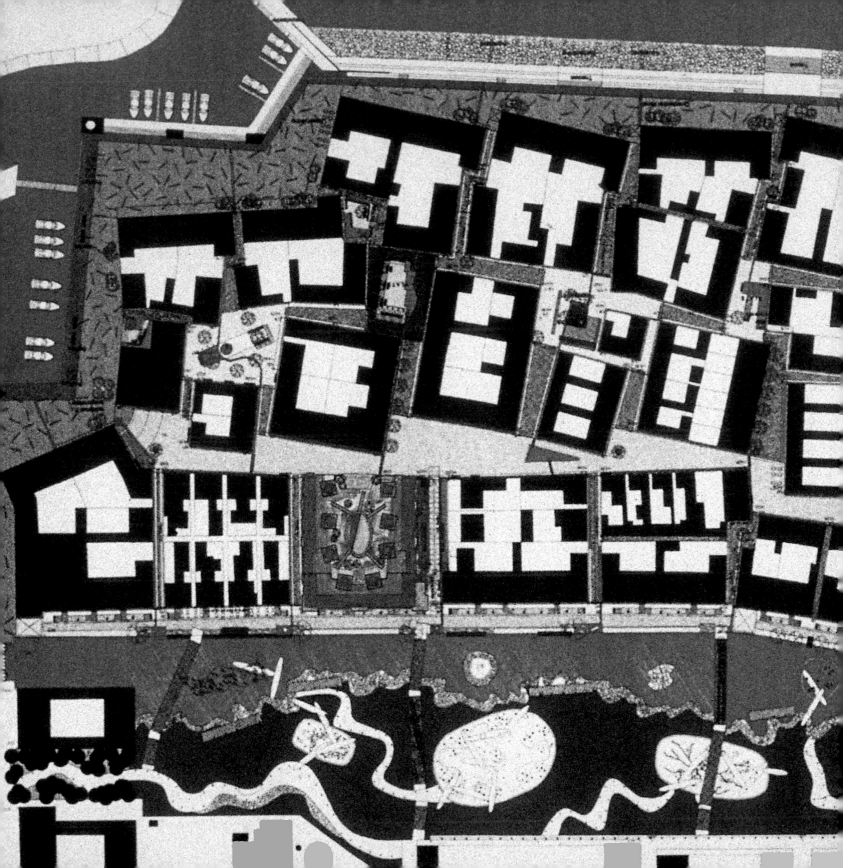

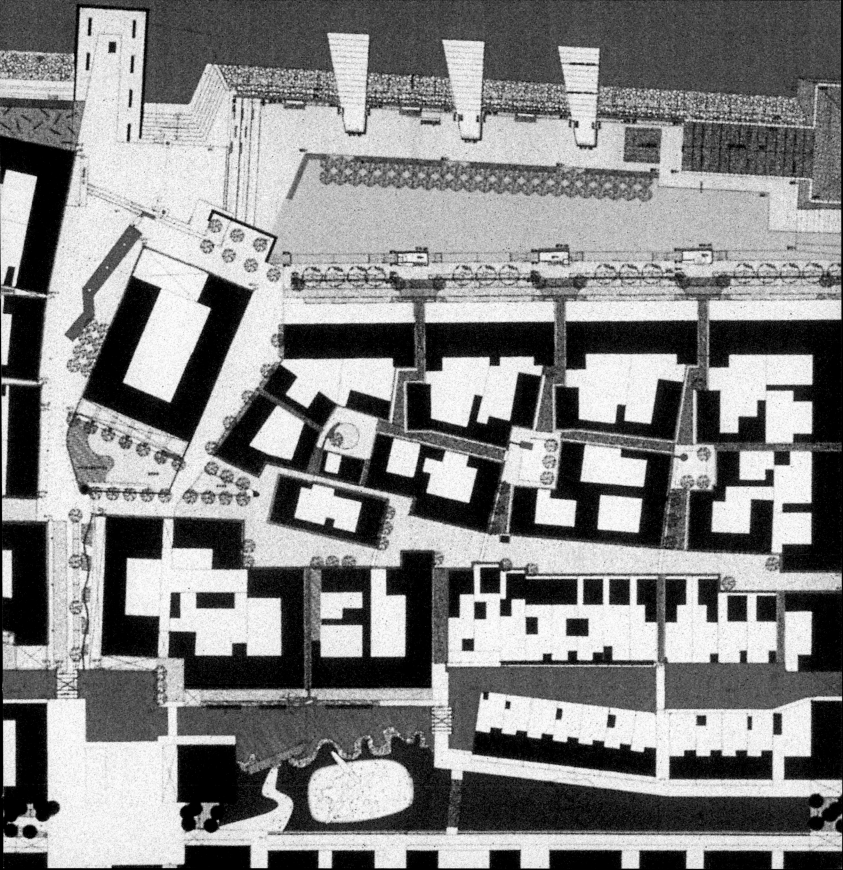

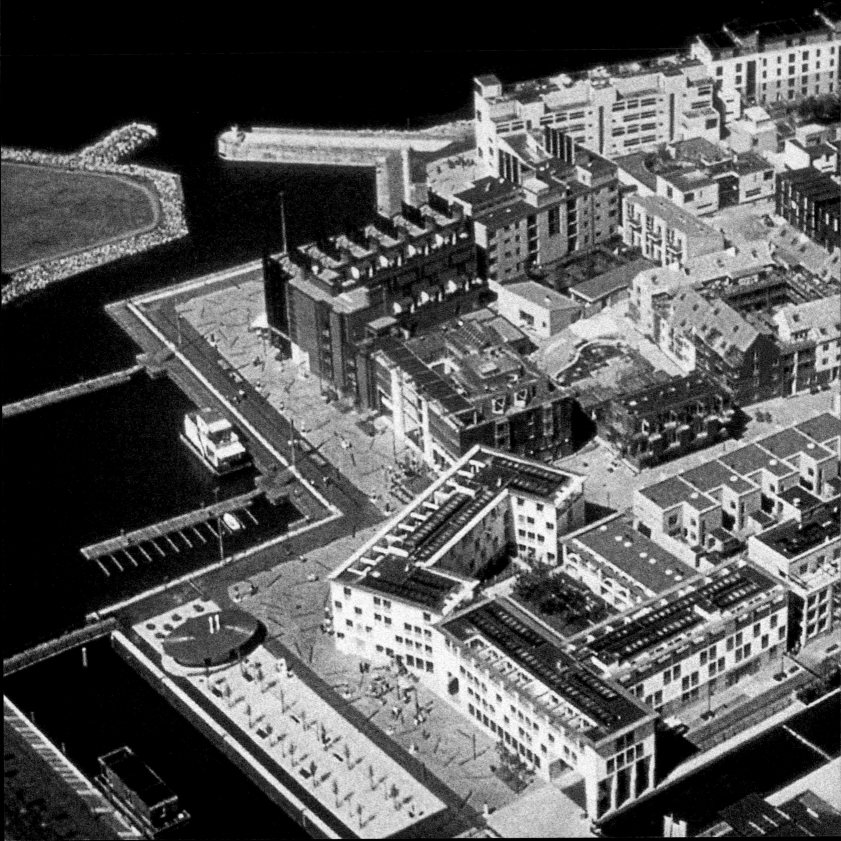

Model of Bo01 Exhibition site.

The Bo01 Housing Exhibition is located on a former industrial site.

Bo01 site plan.

The more discreet architectural treatment of the exterior perimeter façades relates the Tango project to the surrounding urban fabric.

Canal elevation.

The "green-and-wired" building ranges from two-and-a-half to four-and-a-half floors in height, and contains 27 rental apartments, from 600-square-foot studios to 1,950-square-foot three-bedroom units.

MOVEMENT WITHIN A FRAME

SYSTEM OF AN ENVELOPE

The client's challenge for a unique design for each of the units was met by developing a flexible system that articulates the perimeter's exterior elevations while considering the correlation between interior space and its exterior expression. Since the individual units are stacked, the potential for exterior chaos is mediated by a super-order grid that is composed of ribbed precast panels. Textured concrete emphasizes the sense of protection of the outside wall. The weave of alternating horizontal and vertical panels modulates the random placement of windows while responding to the surrounding urban fabric. A contemporary reinterpretation of the traditional ship-lap construction, the louvered texture of the panels captures and reflects the precious northern light while providing a distinct street presence.

This exterior treatment contrasts with the vibrant architectural expression of the shared social space in the interior court. With distant views of the Öresund at higher levels, the living room of each unit occupies part of a tower, projecting inward to "borrow" space from the garden and making the interior units feel more spacious. Likewise, entire walls of glass open onto the garden, allowing the units to literally flow into the landscape.

Within the courtyard, a set of glass pavilions, like small towers, are gathered around a garden, turning slightly as they step around the court—a dance-like movement that inspired Moore Ruble Yudell's Swedish colleagues to give the project its name. Inside, every apartment has a piece of the wall and part of a glass tower—the tower rooms for living, and the wall spaces divided into bedrooms and baths. Each plan for the 27 units is unique, a special combination and shaping of repeated components. Some of the interior walls are moveable to accommodate the individual needs of changing households.

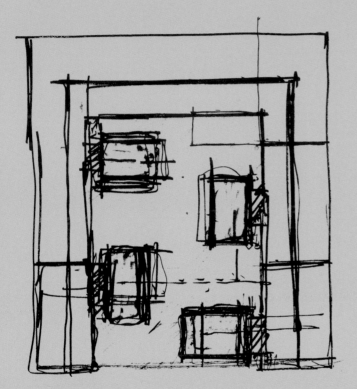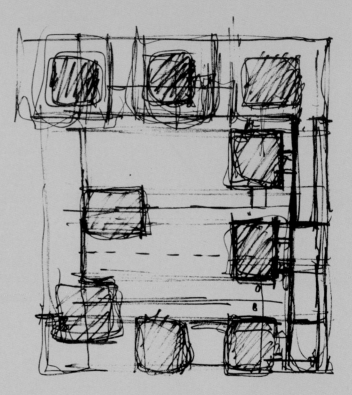

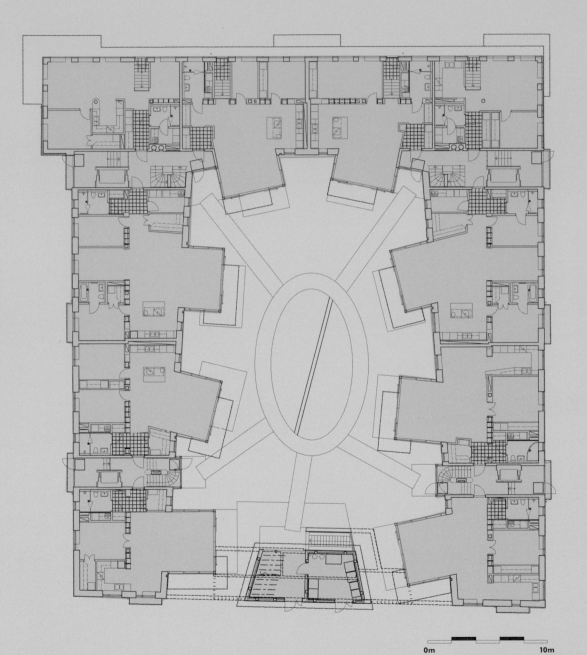

0m   10m

0m   10m

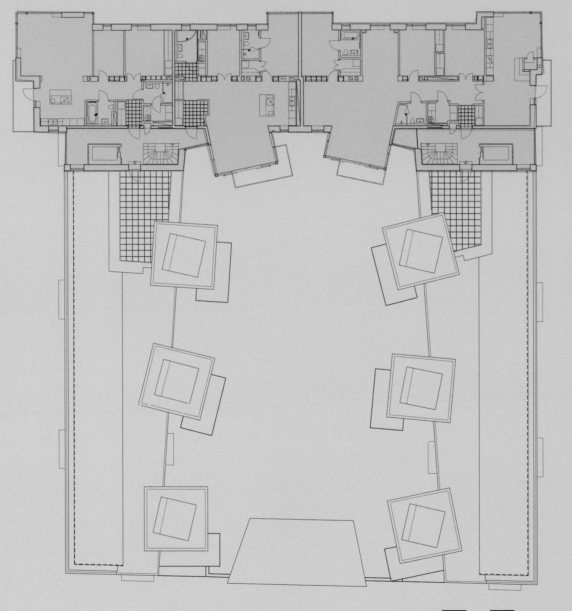

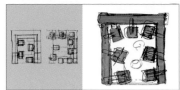

Aerial view of Tango.

Early conceptual design sketches.

Ground floor plan (left) and typical floor plan (right).

Roof plan (left) and Tango model for Swedish Pavilion at 2000 Venice Biennale (right).

The west-facing shared garden, known as "The Yard."

Projecting bays and a syncopated pattern of windows and wall surfaces enliven the exterior façades.

The eastern exterior façade of the building is lined by a canal that runs through the entire Bo01 site.

The louvered texture of ribbed precast panels on the exterior façades captures and reflects sunlight.

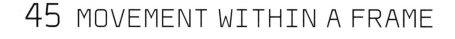

45 MOVEMENT WITHIN A FRAME

SUSTAINABLE TECHNOLOGIES

The Bo01 exhibition strove to demonstrate a sustainable future for urban development. In rehabilitating a classic "brownfield" urban site, the project shows that today's technology can create the city of tomorrow.

TRUMPING THE AUTOMOBILE

As a pedestrian neighborhood, this block was planned to emphasize alternative transportation forms. Planning with a holistic view of environmental matters, inhabitants are inspired to make environmentally friendly decisions in their choice of transportation: walking, bicycling, or taking public transportation. Other than delivery/drop-off areas, there is no designated parking for cars in the Tango complex—the only "parking garage" is for bicycles.

ENERGY SOURCES AND SAVINGS

Bo01's energy concept is based on minimum consumption, renewable resources, and the balance between energy production and consumption, incorporating Sweden's largest urban application of solar energy to date. Energy and drainage systems work together through heat recovery and biogas generation, utilizing the technology of storing heat and coolants in underground reservoirs.

Advanced two-megawatt wind turbines and photovoltaic systems supply electricity. Tango's vacuum tube–insulated solar panels provide sufficient heating and cooling for the entire building. Excess energy is sold to the regional electric company, and then sent back via district heating.

Daylighting and lighting supplement and complement one another. Windows have built-in air vents, bringing fresh air into the apartments throughout the day. Glass areas are triple-glazed to provide insulation. Their R-value, the measure of thermal resistance, is about 6.5, as compared to the 1.5 to 2 for typical American double-paned glass. Two outside layers encapsulate transparent argon gas, forming a "blanket." Two vented inner layers allow fresh air to pass through.

REGENERATING GREEN-SPACE

Planners for Bo01 challenged its developers to set a high standard for green landscape to maintain a healthy ecosystem as integral to the urban environment. A point system evaluated green-space quality; biodiversity, groundwater management, quality of planting materials, and an approved program of landscape maintenance were critical factors in calculating this "green-factor" for each site.

With a nod to traditional Scandinavian sod roofs, Tango's sedum roof surfaces provide additional insulation, replenish oxygen to the atmosphere, and slow runoff during heavy storms. Rainwater is recycled and used to irrigate water gardens. Run-off water is directed into a perimeter channel and then brought into a central cistern and cleaned.

I T AT HOME

In addition to highly sustainable construction materials and great energy conservation, Tango's program integrated state-of-the-art information technology into a residential setting.

An Intelligent Wall, framed of demountable cabinetry, runs through the middle of the plan providing each unit with the cabling and services of a custom-designed information system. Each apartment has its own IT service cupboard, located in or near the kitchen, containing all technology that services the apartment. This system controls and monitors climate, security, and lighting. Tango is also prepared for future supplements and changes to the existing technology.

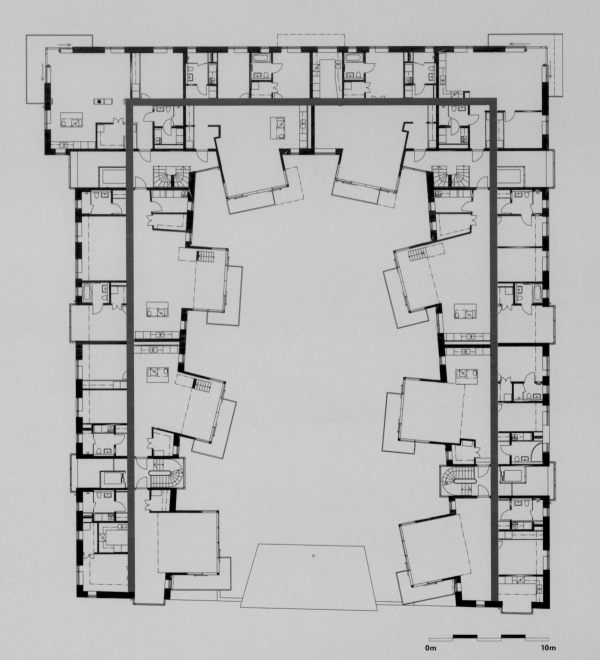

0m   10m

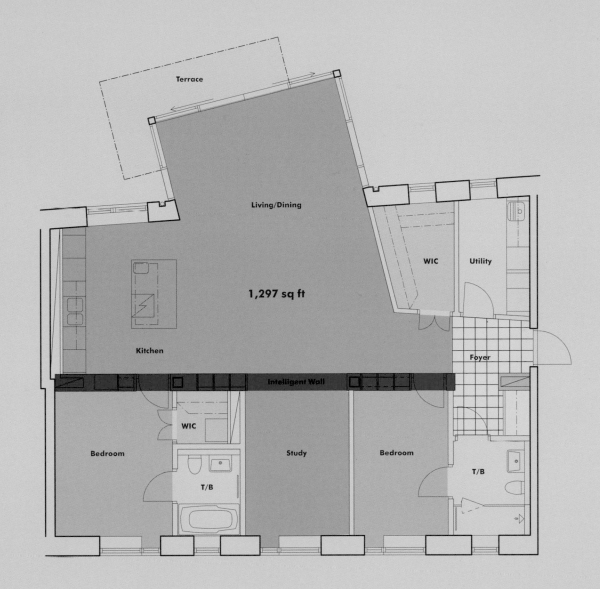

Terrace

Living/Dining

1,297 sq ft

WIC

Utility

Kitchen

Foyer

Intelligent Wall

WIC

Bedroom

Study

Bedroom

T/B

T/B

0m   5m

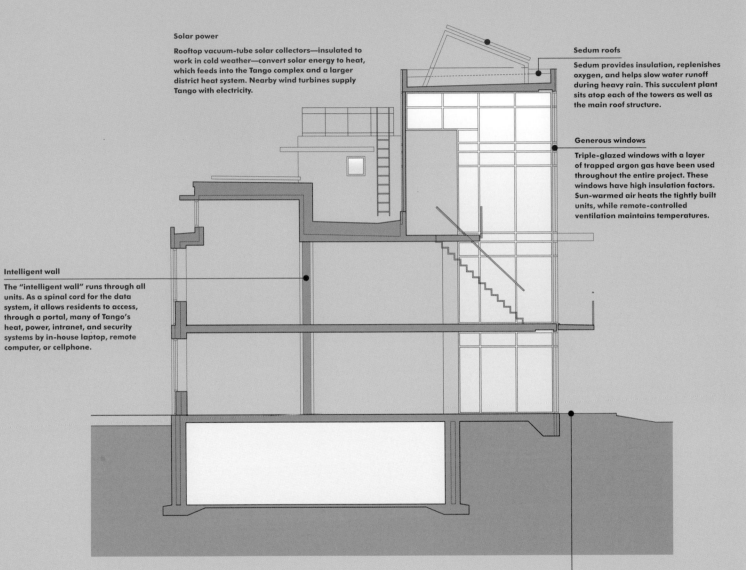

Solar power

Rooftop vacuum-tube solar collectors—insulated to work in cold weather—convert solar energy to heat, which feeds into the Tango complex and a larger district heat system. Nearby wind turbines supply Tango with electricity.

Sedum roofs

Sedum provides insulation, replenishes oxygen, and helps slow water runoff during heavy rain. This succulent plant sits atop each of the towers as well as the main roof structure.

Generous windows

Triple-glazed windows with a layer of trapped argon gas have been used throughout the entire project. These windows have high insulation factors. Sun-warmed air heats the tightly built units, while remote-controlled ventilation maintains temperatures.

Intelligent wall

The "intelligent wall" runs through all units. As a spinal cord for the data system, it allows residents to access, through a portal, many of Tango's heat, power, intranet, and security systems by in-house laptop, remote computer, or cellphone.

Safer soil

Before construction of Tango began, the City of Malmö treated the polluted soil on this former industrial site, then laid five feet of clean soil on top. Around the site, meanwhile, bioremediators (trees and grasses that trap metal and pollutants) bolster the quality of the soil by absorbing toxins.

View framed by the towers.

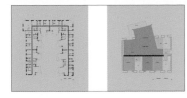

The intelligent wall (left, indicated in red) runs through all the units and supplies a flexible system for media and information technology. Floor plan of a residential unit (right).

Living rooms of the residential units occupy the glazed towers, projecting into the garden to "borrow" green space while making the interior units feel more spacious. Sliding translucent screens provide privacy and shading.

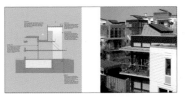

Building section with a description of its sustainable technology features (left). Balcony overlooking pedestrian passageways (right).

Bicycle shed and the exterior street.

Grass-covered surfaces and photovoltaic panels on the roofs provide heating, cooling, and insulation for the building.

Night view of the towers from the courtyard.

COLOR

From the earliest conceptual diagram, color had a powerful role in developing Tango, both in the overall plan and at the scale of the individual units. Color has been so thoroughly integrated into the design that it is inseparable from the building's expression.

On the outside walls that define the block, a syncopated pattern of concrete panels in a quiet palette of neutral colors is intended to integrate into the greater neighborhood. White window frames and the white-painted concrete panels rely on pattern and texture to provide visual interest, complemented by the natural color of zinc paneling and a black granite base.

CHROMATIC CHOREOGRAPHY

Meanwhile the more private interior courtyard towers dance in a riot of strong clear colors. Glassy living room towers emerge from the main mass of the building and rotate at various angles around an elliptical garden courtyard.

The vibrant colors on the towers create a visual separation from the nearly white walls behind them, which are scored in a Mondrian-like pattern of irregular rectangles. Plant materials for the garden were carefully chosen to reinforce the tower colors and to be reminiscent of the marshy wetland that once filled the site.

There was a good deal of discussion regarding whether to put the vibrant color on the expressed metal structure of the living room towers or on the more solid plaster walls. To define each of the towers with a separate color, eight different custom mullion colors of high-tech factory finish were required, at vastly greater expense than just painting the walls. The alternative would have saved money but represented a huge loss to the design. Ultimately, the client agreed that the multi-color mullion approach was intrinsic to the design, and agreed to support the approach despite the additional cost.

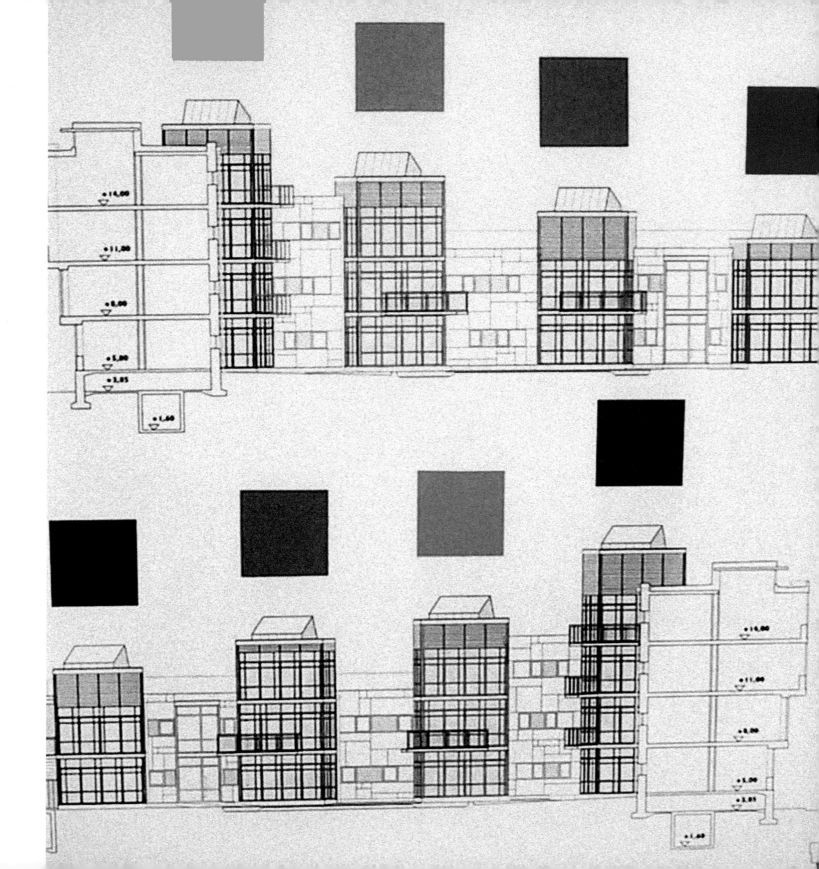

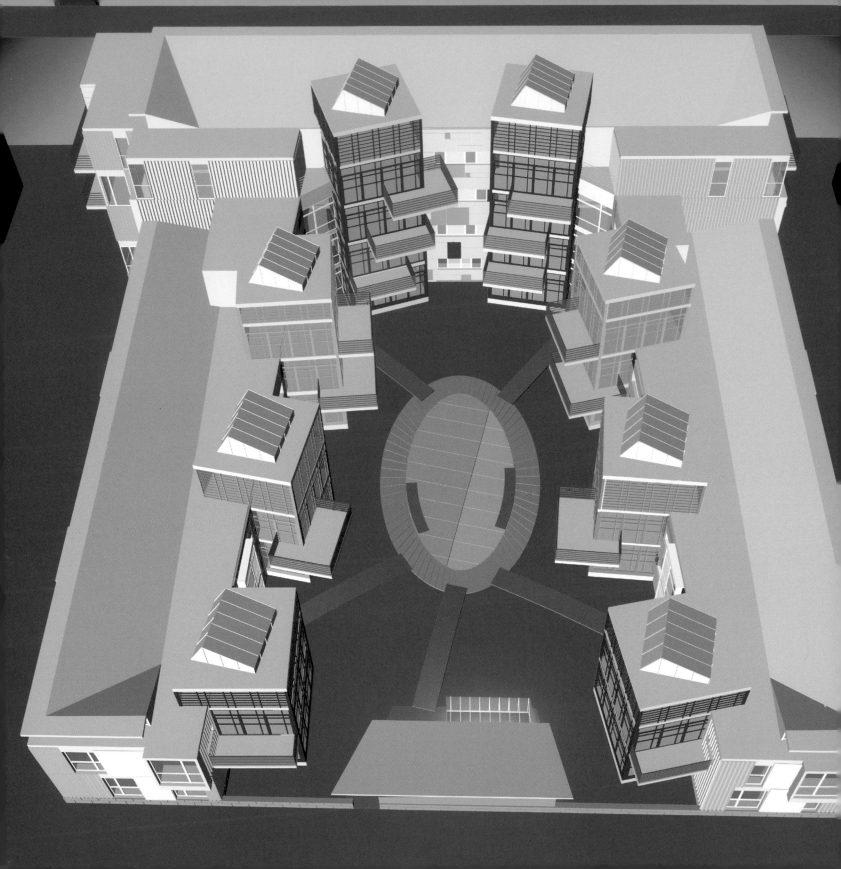

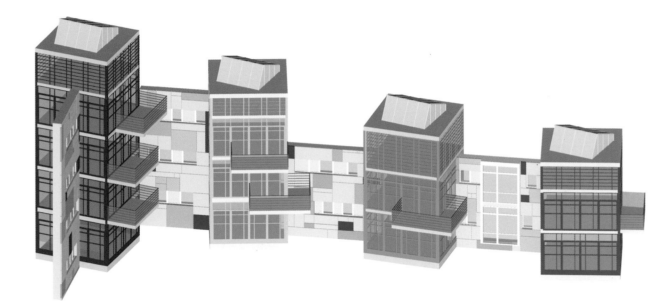

Color conceptual sketch by James Mary O'Connor shows the placement of the towers around the garden.

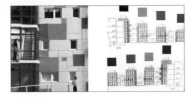

Color studies of the precast concrete panels (left) and the glazed towers facing the garden (right).

Three-dimensional models showing the courtyard and studies for the twisting towers.

The marsh vegetation in the garden is fed by recycled rainwater and provides an ever-changing palette of colors and textures through Malmö's diverse seasons and light conditions.

Living/dining area (left) and studio (right).

The interiors of the residential units feature an appealing palette of complementary materials which were selected according to new green and recyclable guidelines in the district.

Sunlight fills interior rooms, such as this bedroom, through generous windows with views out to the central courtyard.

COMMUNITY AS GARDEN

At the center of the Tango community is a courtyard garden, framed and energized by a vibrant color scheme. Residents can gather informally or formally in this central outdoor space, especially in the summertime. Individual footbridges link the residential cores to the island above an expanse of marshy land that is reminiscent of the geography and flora of the nearby Öresund, lush with grasses, reeds, bamboo, and perennials like darmera, funkia, and ferns. The marsh vegetation is fed by recycled rainwater through manmade streams and a pond made of regular-cut stones and concrete, and the garden provides an ever-changing palette of color and texture through Malmö's diverse seasons and light conditions.

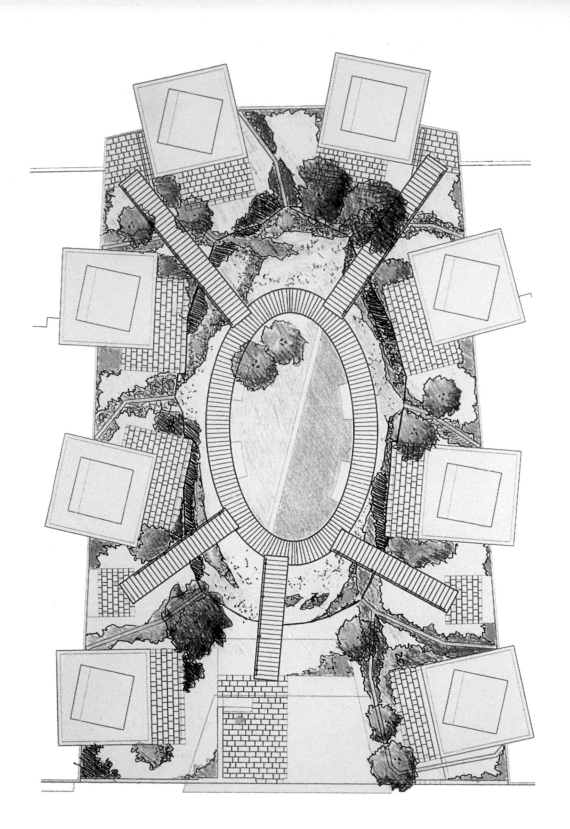

The courtyard garden becomes an impromptu gathering space.

Landscape plan shows the community courtyard with footbridges leading to the central gathering area.

Footbridges link the residential cores to the garden island above an expanse of created marshland.

Towers frame the elliptical courtyard.

The community garden also offers places for contemplation (left). A private balcony overlooks the common courtyard, expanding the spatial qualities of the individual living room (right).

Pedestrian-friendly streets become places for activity and gathering.

This exterior balcony faces west onto the canal-side pedestrian passage.

The block is primarily accessed by pedestrian and bicycle traffic.

At night, the glowing towers impart a sense of welcome and security in the courtyard.

HISTORY

In 1977, Moore Ruble Yudell began much the same way that it currently works—as a spirited collaboration among partners and associates. From the beginning, the founding partners—Charles Moore, John Ruble, and Buzz Yudell—shared a passion for an original architecture that grows out of an intense dialogue with places and people, celebrating human activity while enhancing and nurturing community. These shared passions and concerns continue in both the manner of work and the places ultimately crafted, balancing a collective commitment to humanistic architecture with the energy of individual initiatives.

Moore Ruble Yudell's work began with noted residential designs like the Rodes House, and quickly evolved into a broad spectrum of public and private projects. With Saint Matthew's Church in 1979, the work in institutional and cultural places began to characterize the practice. A win in a major design competition for Berlin's Tegel Harbor in 1980 vaulted the small firm into an international practice centered on housing, community planning, and mixed-use urban projects of all kinds. The international and particularly European and Asian work led to increased awareness of issues in sustainability, social housing, construction practices, and the need to work collaboratively with complex teams of clients and consultants.

Since 1985, Buzz Yudell and John Ruble have led the firm, supported and complemented by a multi-talented and collegial group of principals and senior associates. The firm's wide-ranging interests and enthusiasms continue to evolve, guided by ideals and formal strategies that, as architectural writer Sally Woodbridge once remarked, have become "community property." Demonstrated skill in urban design and master-planning, as well as the art and craft of building design, has allowed Moore Ruble Yudell to work successfully on a broad range of building types around the globe, including civic and cultural, institutional, technological and research, as well as mixed-use and housing.

CREDITS

OWNER
MKB Fastighets AB, Malmö, Sweden
Lars Birve, Ingvar Carlsson, Allan Karlsson,
Caroline Ullman-Hammer, Olle Berglind

DESIGN ARCHITECTS
Moore Ruble Yudell Architects & Planners
with SWECO FFNS Arkitekter AB
Partner-in-Charge: John Ruble, FAIA
Partner: Buzz Yudell, FAIA
Principal-in-Charge/
Project Architect: James Mary O'Connor, AIA
Project Team: Lisa Belian, Tony Tran
Colors and Materials: Tina Beebe, Kaoru Orime
Landscape Design: John Ruble,
James Mary O'Connor, Tina Beebe
Interior Design, Exhibition Apartment:
Tina Beebe, Kaoru Orime
Digital Renderings: Ross Morishige
Models: Mark Grand, Chad T. Takenaka,
Vely Zajec, Don Hornbeck, Joshua Lunn,
Matthew Vincent, Lance Collins

EXECUTIVE ARCHITECTS
SWECO FFNS Arkitekter AB
Principal Architect: Bertil Öhrström
Project Architects: Karin Bellander, Lars Lindahl
Project Team: Anna Hessle,
Johanna Wittenmark, Robert Arvidsson
Landscape Architects: Siv Degerman,
Mats Johansson
Interior Designers: Karin Bellander,
Johanna Wittenmark

LANDSCAPE ARCHITECTS
Moore Ruble Yudell Architects & Planners
with SWECO FFNS Arkitekter AB

PHOTOGRAPHERS
Werner Huthmacher, Ole Jais, Kim Zwarts

PROJECT MANAGEMENT
SWECO Projektledning AB, Malmö, Sweden
Nils Johansson, Anders Landsbo,
Pär Hammarberg

GENERAL CONTRACTOR
Thage Anderssons Byggnads AB,
Tollarp, Sweden

BIOGRAPHIES

JOHN RUBLE, FAIA, PARTNER
John Ruble began his career as architect and planner in the Peace Corps in Tunisia, where a profound experience of culture, climate, and place provided lasting influences on his work. With Princeton, New Jersey, architect Jules Gregory, he designed a series of award-winning public schools and civic projects before moving to California in 1974. With architecture degrees from the University of Virginia and UCLA's School of Architecture and Urban Planning, John has also been active in teaching and research, leading graduate design studios at UCLA and Cornell University. At UCLA, he studied and associated with Charles Moore, joining Moore and Buzz Yudell in partnership in 1977.

Working closely with partner Buzz Yudell, John has helped to shape the firm's humanistic and inclusive approach to design, translating their deep concerns for human habitation and interaction into architecture and planning at many scales. His breadth and depth of experience in the design of both social housing and market-based residential and mixed-use urban projects has ranged from local to international sites. As Moore Ruble Yudell's portfolio has expanded into new areas of expertise—from social housing to embassies— John has sought to make each work part of a broad, sustained exploration in the creation of place.

BUZZ YUDELL, FAIA, PARTNER
Buzz Yudell's passion for architecture grew out of a synthesis of artistic and social concerns. At Yale College, his work in sculpture was complemented by his exploration of the sciences and humanities. Graduate study at Yale expanded these commitments to a range of scales from small constructions in situ to urban design. Here he began his long association with Charles Moore. In 1977 Buzz joined Charles and John Ruble in a partnership based on shared humanistic values and a celebration of collaboration within the office and beyond to their clients and communities.

Buzz has collaborated intensively with John to expand the firm's expression and expertise to campus, cultural, civic, and residential architecture. His commitment to creating humane places inspired by climatic and cultural understanding has informed the firm's work at many scales. Buzz continues to be as interested in the design and craft of lighting and furniture as in planning for urban infill or sustainable growth. His strong interest in the house as the quantum of community has helped to create a body of timeless residential work. His interest in nurturing community has found fresh expression on numerous campuses including UCLA, UCSB, Cal Tech, University of Cincinnati, Dartmouth, and MIT. Throughout his career, teaching, research, writing, and community service have been critical to the evolution and exploration of both the theoretical and physical role of architecture in shaping and celebrating place and community.

JAMES MARY O'CONNOR, AIA, PRINCIPAL
Born in Dublin, Ireland, James Mary O'Connor came to Charles Moore's Master Studios at UCLA in 1982 as a Fulbright Scholar. James received his Bachelor of Science in Architecture degree from Trinity College, Dublin, his Diploma in Architecture from the Dublin Institute of Technology, and his Master of Architecture from UCLA.

James has provided spirited design and project management for residential, academic, and mixed-use urban projects, including

Kobe Nishiokamoto Housing in Japan; the Horace Mann Elementary School and Fairmont Towers Hotel Addition, both in San Jose, California; and the 606 Broadway housing complex in Santa Monica, California. International work has become a focus, with large-scale housing and planning projects such as the Potatisåkern and Tango projects in Malmö, Sweden; the Serendra mixed-use development for 5,000 housing units in Manila, Philippines; ChunSenBian Housing in Chongqing, China; and Tianjin-Xinhe New Town in Tianjin, China. His interest in uncommon building types is reflected in the Sunlaw Power Plant Prototype in Los Angeles, and the Santa Monica Civic Center Parking Structure. With irrepressible energy, James has also led Moore Ruble Yudell teams in national and international design competitions, such as the Beijing Wanhao Century Center and the winning design for the Clarice Smith Performing Arts Center in College Park, Maryland.

Over the past 15 years, James has taught design studios, lectured, and been invited as guest critic at UCLA, USC, SCI-Arc, the University of Calgary–Alberta, the University of Hawaii–Manoa, Ball State University College of Architecture & Planning in Muncie, Indiana, Hong-Ik University Department of Architecture in Seoul, Korea, and the following schools in China: Tianjin University School of Architecture, Tongji University School of Architecture in Shanghai, Southeast University School of Architecture in Nanjing, and Chongqing University School of Architecture.

TINA BEEBE, COLOR AND MATERIALS
Tina Beebe received her MFA from the Yale School of Art and Architecture. Working with Charles Moore as a student, Tina joined his firm in Essex, Connecticut, and subsequently came to California to work with him in 1976. She also worked in the office of Charles and Ray Eames, learning much from her great friend and mentor, Ray Eames. As resident colorist for Moore Ruble Yudell, Tina integrates these influences with her extensive travel experiences to inform her choices for custom color and material palette. She has provided consulting services for many distinguished U.S. and international architecture firms.

Tina's practice has expanded to combine her design and color abilities to include the design of residential and commercial gardens. As plant material inspires her color palette, color evokes ideas for whole gardens, which in turn complement and enhance the color and materials of architecture.

ACKNOWLEDGMENTS

A NOTE FROM MOORE RUBLE YUDELL
We wish to thank Anthony Iannacci and Edizioni Press for this opportunity to extend the unique story of Tango to a larger audience. Editors Aaron Seward and Sarah Palmer have provided a particularly effective format in which to present the qualities of a single building, and the graphic design by Project Projects offers a new way of seeing Tango's spirited complexity.

At the core of the book is Michael Webb's well-researched piece on the creative process that resulted in Tango. He has accurately captured the excitement and energy that shaped the design from the start, and gives a sense of the unusual goals and standards with which our enlightened clients at MKB approached the housing exhibition at Bo01. Moreover, he also provides a sense of the creative lifestyle of Tango's inhabitants.

Tango was an exceptional challenge and a wonderful experience for all of us who worked together on its design and realization. At SWECO FFNS our "partners" Bertil Öhrström, Lars Lindahl, and Karin Bellander joined us equally in the vision of the project, which quickly acquired a life of its own, guided, nurtured, and energized continuously by James Mary O'Connor. As the work evolved, Tina Beebe and Kaoru Orime gave the design its special trajectory through a unique and powerful color idea, and, if that were not enough, Tina and Siv Degerman of FFNS went even further in establishing the garden design of the courtyard.

Most of all, this book presents the project through the eyes of the gifted Berlin photographer Werner Huthmacher, whose work finds not only the work's iconic moments, but the whimsy and, we like to think, charm of the unexpected. Additional views of the exhibition unit's interior by Ole Jais convey a story of habitation.

Our own editor for the design and production of this monograph, Ken Kim, has made countless contributions to both content and quality, assisted by Janet Sager, Rebecca Bubenas, and Tony Tran.

Finally, we wish to acknowledge the courage and imagination of those who have come to live in Tango—they are the active inhabitants to whom this and all our work is dedicated.